IT'S A JUNGLE OUT THERE!

JUNGLE ANIMALS FOR KIDS

Children's Environment Books

Speedy Publishing LLC

40 E. Main St. #1156

Newark, DE 19711

www.speedypublishing.com

Copyright 2017

Visit

BABY PROFESSOR
EDUCATION KIDS

www.BabyProfessorBooks.com

to download Free Baby Professor eBooks
and view our catalog of new and exciting
Children's Books

For us, a jungle is a tangle of wild growth. It is hard to get through, where we don't know what might be creeping up on us. For other creatures, the jungle is home! Let's find out about some of them.

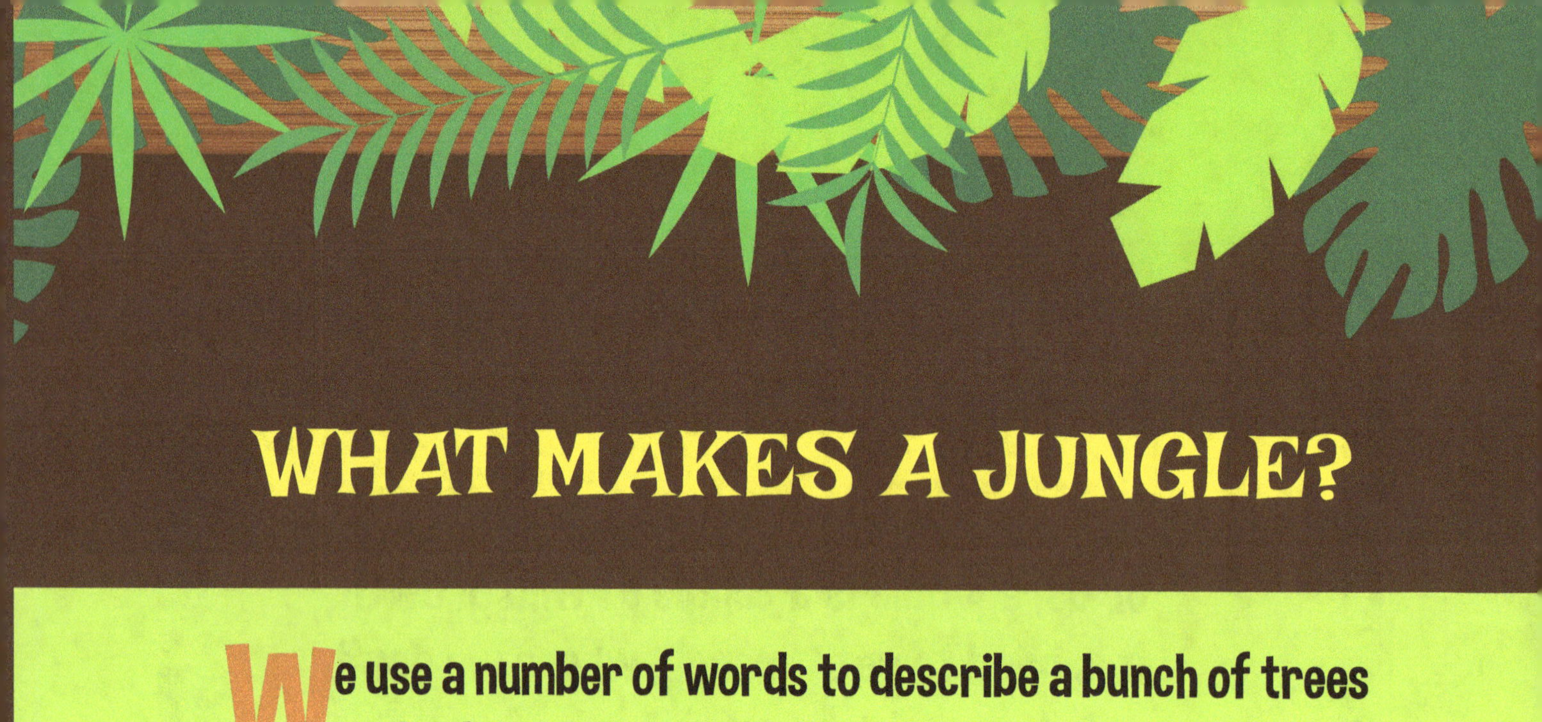

WHAT MAKES A JUNGLE?

We use a number of words to describe a bunch of trees and other growing plants.

- A **forest** is an area with a high density of trees.

- A jungle is a forest area where the temperature is warm and there is a lot of vegetation. Lots of sunlight reaches the ground, so a lot of smaller trees and plants can grow and tangle together. It can be pretty hard to walk through a jungle!

🌼 A **copse** or a **grove** is a few trees in a group. Usually you can see past the tree trunks to clear land beyond.

🌼 A **rain forest** is a forest that has at least 60 inches of rainfall a year. Tropical rain forests rarely get cool, while rain forests away from the equator can even see snow at times.

Rain forests have a thick canopy of tree growth, so little sunlight makes its way to the forest floor. Not a lot of small plants grow between the trees because they can't get enough sunlight, so walking in a rain forest is usually fairly easy.

The edge of a rain forest can be a lot like a jungle, and of course for the animals who live there what humans call where they live doesn't matter! Let's visit with some animals we might run into in a jungle.

JUNGLE GREAT APES

All of the great apes except for humans live in jungles, and all of the non-human ones except for orangutans live in Africa. The orangutan's home is the jungles of Borneo and Sumatra. Orangutans spend most of their lives high in trees, and are the largest animals who live that way.

CHIMPANZEE

CHIMPANZEES

Chimpanzees and eastern lowland gorillas live in heavy forests at the edge of true jungles, and the chimpanzees spend a lot of time in the open savanna as well. The larger great apes like the eastern mountain gorillas, live in jungles in central Africa.

Humans continue to cut down forests and jungles for their wood to open up land for farming, mining, roads, and other purposes. Loss of habitat is threatening all of the great apes (except humans) with extinction.

LION

JUNGLE CATS

We call the lion "the king of the jungle", but that is not where most of them live. Of more than 20,000 lions of all species, only about 300 Asiatic lions (an endangered species) live in jungles, in India.

However, many of the large cats live and hunt in the jungles. Where they live, they are usually the top predators. You could meet Bengal tigers, leopards, and jaguars in jungles of Africa and Asia. You can read about the large cats in the Baby Professor book **My Pet Cat Has Wild Cousins.**

TIGER

Leopards are excellent tree climbers, and hunt monkeys among the branches. They also lie in wait on low branches above trails through the jungle, and then drop down on an animal passing below.

Leopards also hang in trees partially-eaten carcasses of animals they have killed, so they can come back and have a snack later on.

FOREST ELEPHANTS

Most elephants live in the open savanna or in woodlands near the edge of open areas. However, there is one species, the forest elephant, that is at home in forests and even jungles. Forest elephants are much smaller than their cousins that we see in movies and in circuses. They grow to about eight feet high at the shoulder, so they can get through forested areas without too much trouble.

ELEPHANT

They live in smaller groups than the elephants of the savanna do, and eat a diet with a wider range of foods because there are more different edible plants in the rain forest than in the savanna.

Without forest elephants, jungle plants would have a harder time surviving. The elephants are a significant source of fertilizer, and also transport seeds from the masses of fruit that they eat so that the seeds can take root in soil that is not right under their parent tree.

GLASS FROG

JUNGLE-DWELLERS IN SOUTH AMERICA

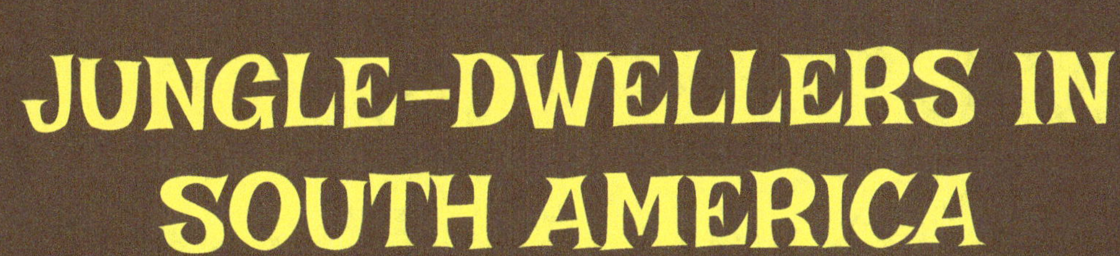

Here are some neat animals who live in the jungles and rain forests of South America:

Glass frog

This frog lives like most other frogs, but it has a distinctive look. Its skin is so transparent you can see its internal organs at work, including its beating heart.

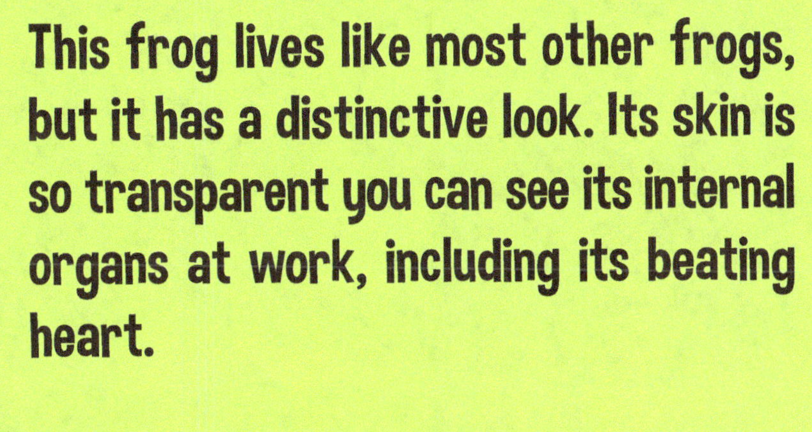

Toucan

Toucans have an amazing, colorful bill. Many jungle and rain forest birds wear bright feathers, but not many have bright beaks!

SPIDER MONKEY

Spider monkey

The spider monkey lives high in rain forest and jungle trees, swinging gracefully through the canopy of the forest. They are often so high up that people walking below rarely have a chance to see them.

Kinkajou

The kinkajou is also called a honey bear. It is like a golden raccoon, and has a long tail that helps it hold on to branches as it moves among forest trees.

Mata Mata

The Mata Mata is a rain forest turtle with a long neck. It feeds on fish, sucking them through its mouth and directly to its stomach without any chewing necessary.

CAPYBARA

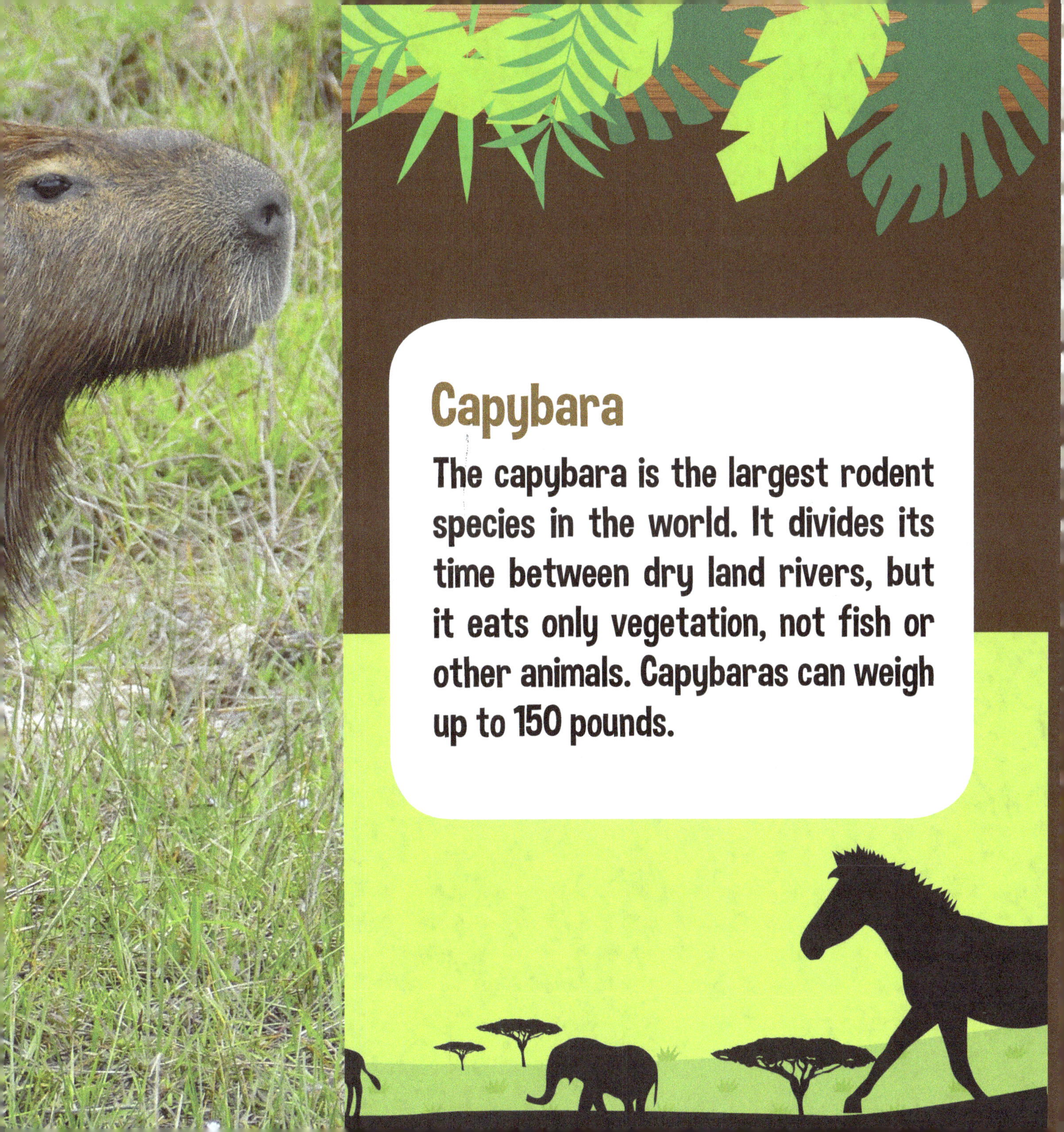

Capybara

The capybara is the largest rodent species in the world. It divides its time between dry land rivers, but it eats only vegetation, not fish or other animals. Capybaras can weigh up to 150 pounds.

Poison Dart frog

This little frog looks very pretty, but it is also very dangerous. If you touched its skin just with your finger, you could absorb enough poison from the frog to kill you.

Anaconda

Green anacondas are the largest snakes in the world, growing as long as 30 feet and weighing as much as 550 pounds. They kill their prey by wrapping themselves around it and squeezing it until it stops breathing. Anacondas attack and eat prey as large and agile as deer, jaguars and caiman.

Black caiman

The black caiman is like a super-alligator. It can grow to twenty feet long, and has a stronger bite than Nile crocodiles. Caimans like to eat almost everything else that lives in the jungle, including deer, monkeys, fish and snakes.

Central Africa has deep and varied jungles. Here are some of the creatures that live there:

- Colobus monkey
- Honey badger
- Bush viper
- Aye-Aye
- Aardvark

AFROMONTANE INDIGENOUS FOREST
OF SOUTH AFRICA

Colobus monkey

"Colobus" comes from a Greek word for "wounded", and the monkeys got this name because, unlike other primates, they do not have thumbs. However, not having thumbs seems to let them move more surely through the trees. They may lack thumbs, but they have an extra-long tail that helps them with their balance. They spend almost all their lives high in the trees of thick forests.

Honey badger

The honey badger looks like a cuddly pet, but it is a violent, aggressive fighter. Honey badgers willingly attack even lions, buffaloes, and people. They can bite very hard, and hate to retreat or run away.

Even though honey badgers are great attackers, they get their name from their love of honey. They follow a honey-loving bird called the honey guide to locate bees' nests in the forest.

Honey badgers are also tool users! They use sticks, stones, and even logs to help them break open nests so they can get at more honey.

Bush viper

Bush vipers spend days on top of flowering bushes, soaking in warmth from the sun. Then at night they lurk in trees, waiting for something to come past that they can attack. They can change the color of their skin to blend in with their surroundings.

The viper's head is bigger than its neck, so it looks truly scary. Bush vipers avoid where people live, which is a good thing. The venom in their bite can be fatal, and so far there is no remedy for it.

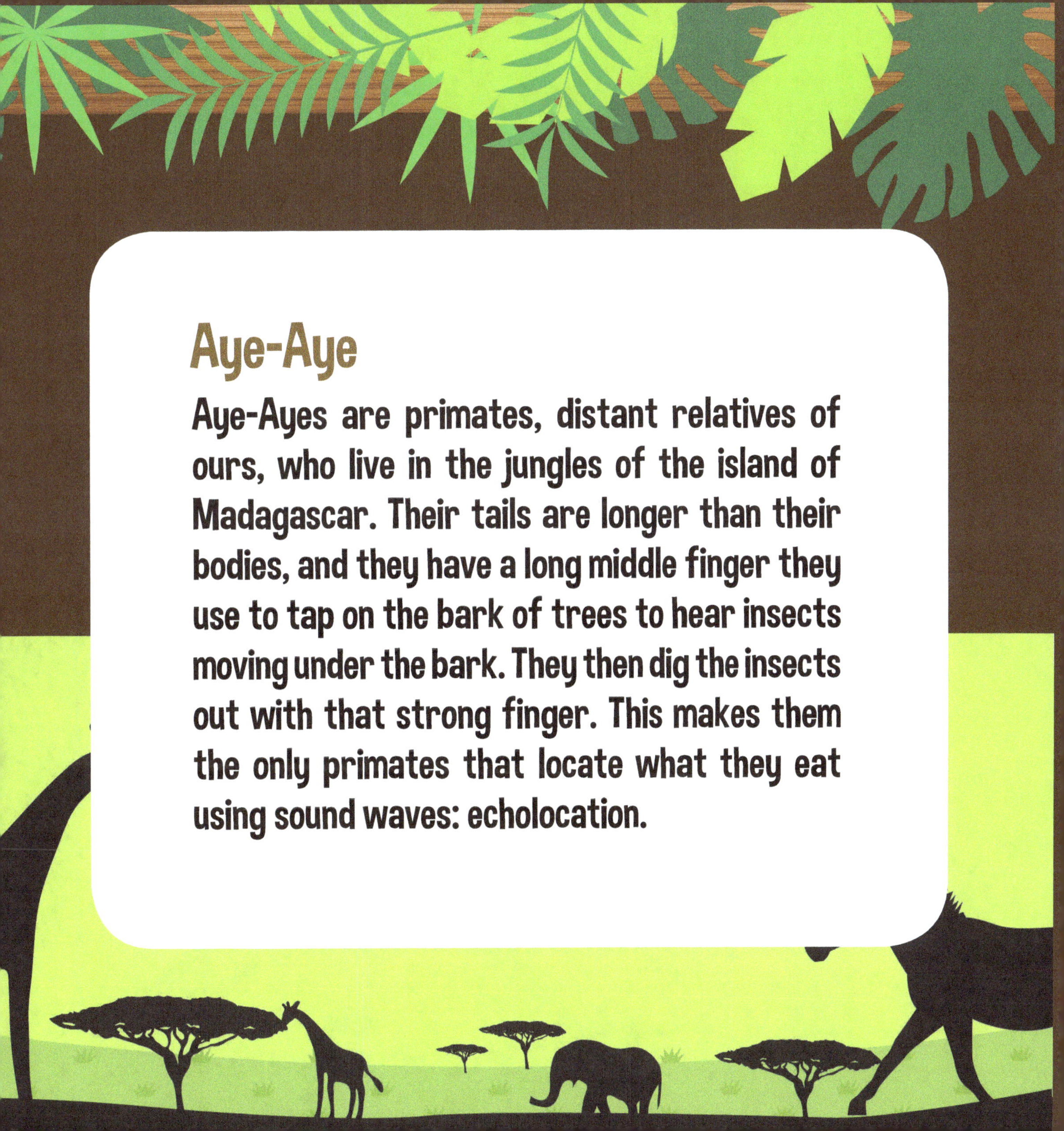

Aye-Aye

Aye-Ayes are primates, distant relatives of ours, who live in the jungles of the island of Madagascar. Their tails are longer than their bodies, and they have a long middle finger they use to tap on the bark of trees to hear insects moving under the bark. They then dig the insects out with that strong finger. This makes them the only primates that locate what they eat using sound waves: echolocation.

Aardvark

Aardvarks look like they have borrowed body parts from many different creatures. They have snouts like pigs, ears like rabbits, and a tail like a kangaroo. And their closest relatives are elephants!

Aardvarks hunt at night for termites and ants, and they live wherever these insects live. They move from termite mound to anthill, digging their way into nests.

These creatures have long, sticky tongues that they insert into an insect nest, dragging out as many as one hundred insects at a time. They can eat over 50,000 ants in one meal. Their claws are sharp and powerful, but they don't attack other animals.

AADVARK

A WORLD OF WONDERFUL ANIMALS

All around us are amazing creatures, fellow residents of this Earth. Learn more about them in Baby Professor books like *The Great White Shark, The World's Most Beautiful Birds,* and *Vulnerable, Endangered, and Critically Endangered Animals.*

Visit
BABY PROFESSOR
EDUCATION KIDS
www.BabyProfessorBooks.com
to download Free Baby Professor eBooks
and view our catalog of new and exciting
Children's Books